YOU CAN TEACH YOURSELF®

UKE

by William Bay

Online Audio & Video

Audio
www.melbay.com/94809EB

Video
dv.melbay.com/94809

You Tube
www.melbay.com/94809V

Audio Contents

WWW.MELBAY.COM

Contents

How To Hold The Uke

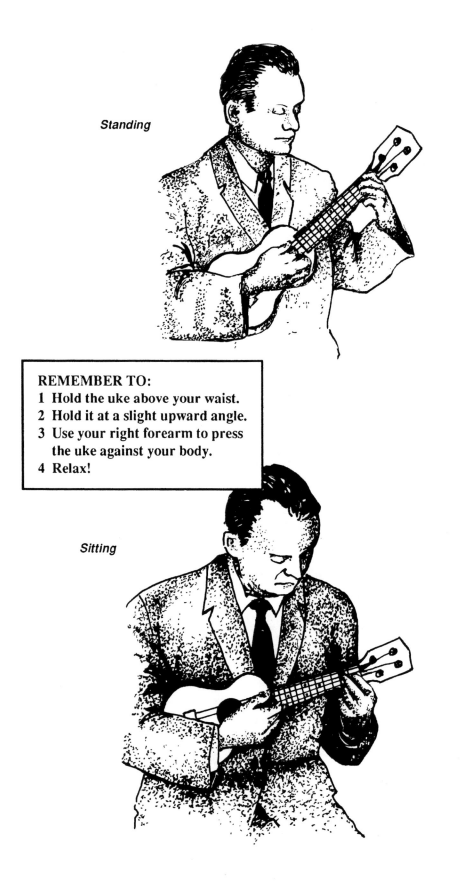

Standing

REMEMBER TO:
1 Hold the uke above your waist.
2 Hold it at a slight upward angle.
3 Use your right forearm to press the uke against your body.
4 Relax!

Sitting

Parts Of The Uke

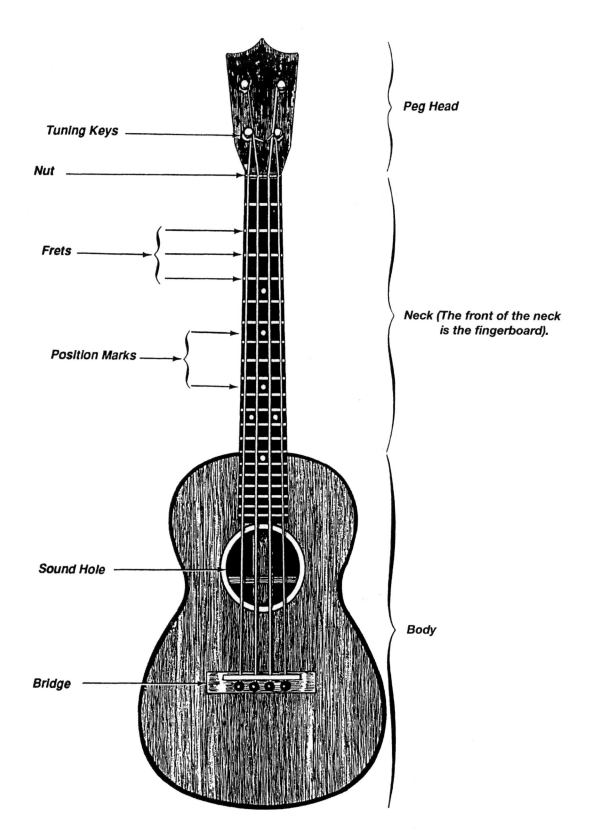

Peg Head

Tuning Keys

Nut

Frets

Neck (The front of the neck
is the fingerboard).

Position Marks

Sound Hole

Body

Bridge

Ways To Tune Your Uke

1. Tune It To A Piano

This method will use *"C tuning."* In C tuning the strings are tuned to the following notes:

First String . . . . A ①
Second String . . . . . . E ②
Third String . . . . C ③
Fourth String . . . . . . G ④

On a piano the notes are found as follows:

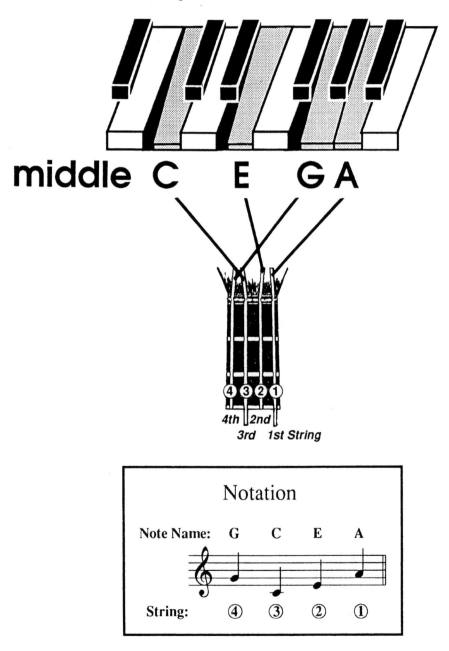

2. Tuning With A Pitch Pipe

Ukulele pitch pipes can be purchased from most music stores. Blow into the appropriate sound hole and tune the string to the correct pitch.

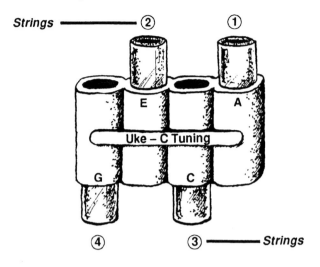

3. Tuning By Ear

Once you tune your first string to a pitch that sounds correct (not too high or too low), you can use the following expression:

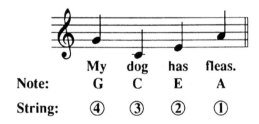

	My	dog	has	fleas.
Note:	G	C	E	A
String:	④	③	②	①

Important Hint

There is usually a tiny screw in the back of each tuning peg. Be sure each screw is tight. If they are loose, the strings will slip, and you will not be able to tune the uke. (Do not tighten them, however, so tight that the tuning peg will not turn!)

Peg-Tightening Screw

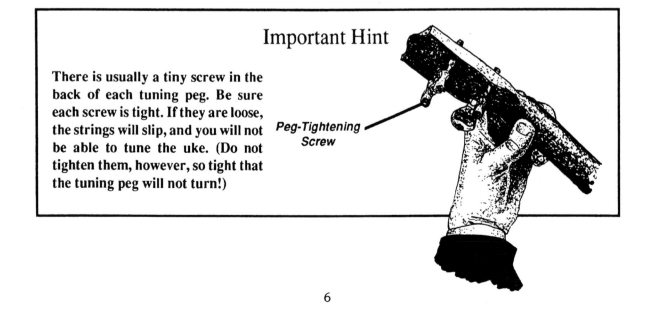

Strumming Your Uke

1. Using A Pick

Picks can be purchased at your local music store. It is usually desirable to use a "felt" pick. This will give your uke a soft, mellow tone. Plastic picks will give a sharper, more brittle tone. If a plastic pick is to be used, try to find a thin, very flexible one.

Felt Pick

Holding The Pick (Right Hand)

2. Using Your Thumb

You can also strum your uke with your right-hand thumb.

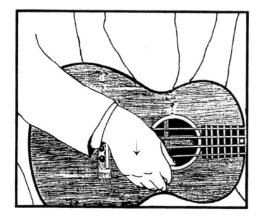

Down Strum ↓

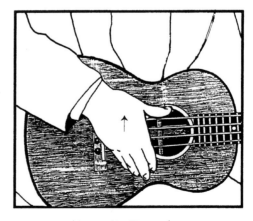

Up Strum ↑

The Left Hand

The following illustrations show the proper positioning of the left hand. Notice that only the *tips* of the left-hand fingers are used to press down the strings. (Be sure your fingers do not accidentally touch the adjacent string. If this happens, the adjacent string will sound muffled or deadened.) Be sure the thumb is on the back of the neck, *not* wrapped around the side. Finally, when you press down a string, place your finger behind the metal fret, *not* on top of it.

Correct

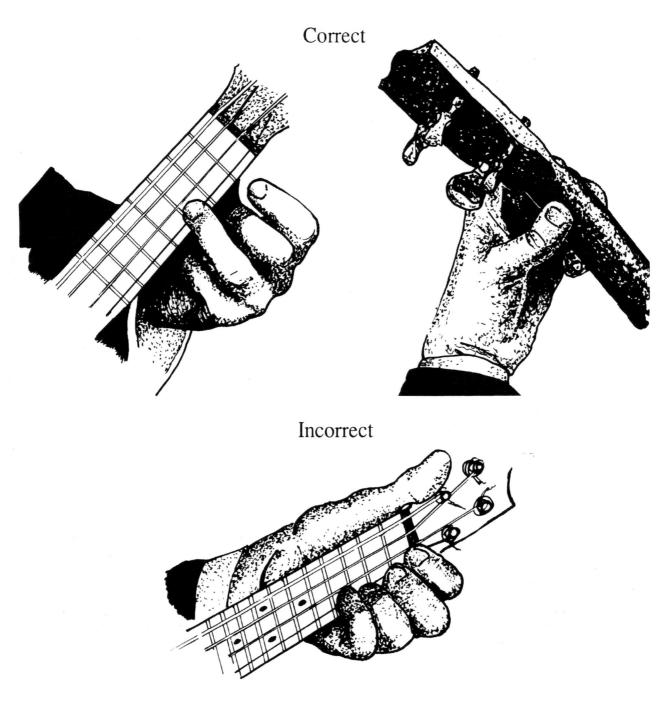

Incorrect

How To Read Chord Diagrams

A chord diagram shows you where to place your fingers in order to play a chord. The vertical lines are the strings. The horizontal lines are the frets. The circled numbers are left-hand fingers.

Left-hand fingers are numbered as follows:

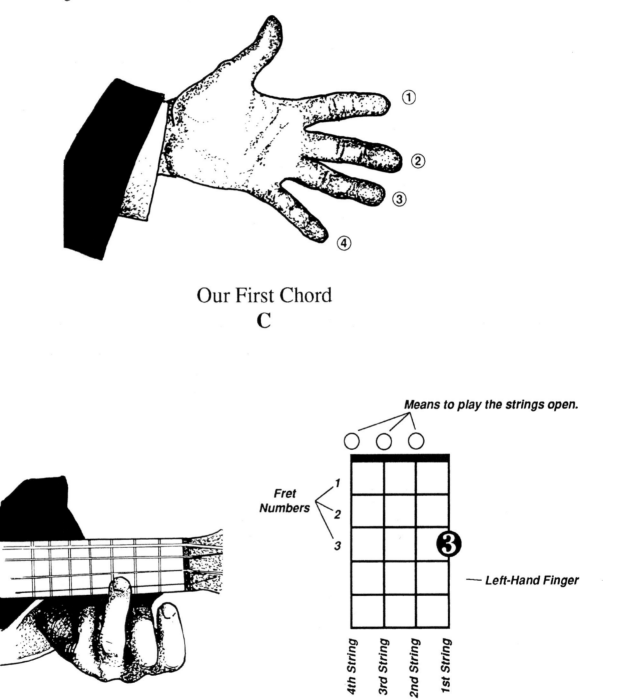

Our First Chord
C

Playing The C Chord

Practice strumming the C chord until it sounds clear.

Time Signatures

Every song has a time signature. The time signature appears at the beginning of every song and tells you how many beats or counts are in each measure.

$\frac{4}{4}$ or **C** = "Common Time"

Hold the C chord and play as follows.

Remember: / = Down Strum

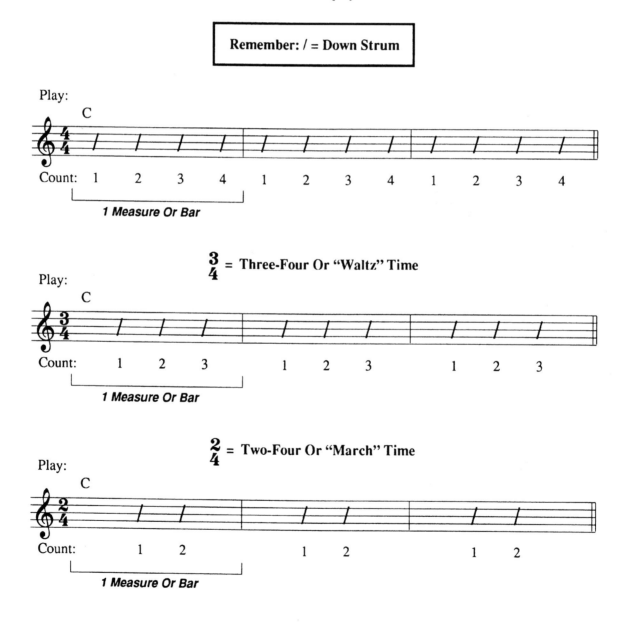

Our First Songs

Reading Music

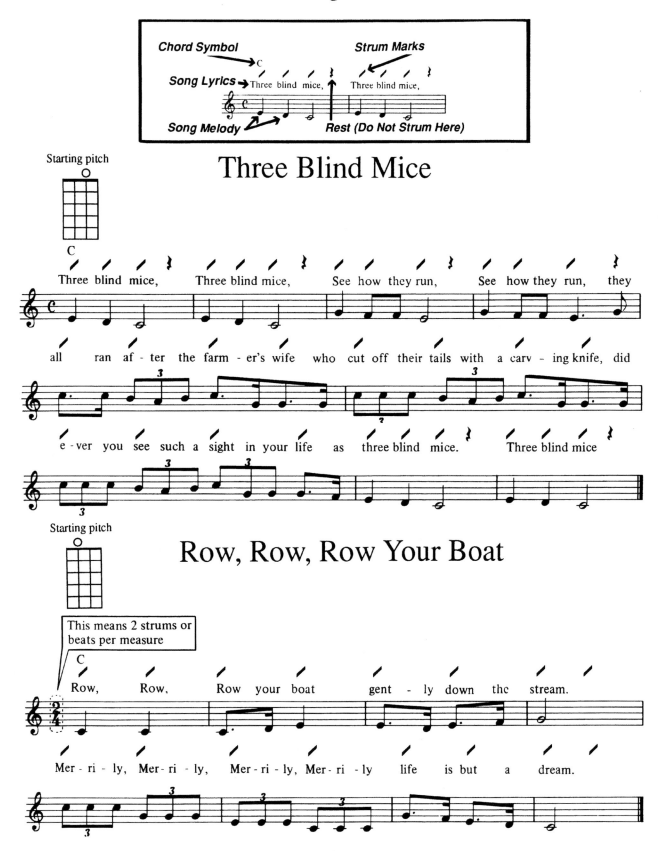

Three Blind Mice

Three blind mice, Three blind mice, See how they run, See how they run, they all ran af - ter the farm - er's wife who cut off their tails with a carv - ing knife, did e - ver you see such a sight in your life as three blind mice. Three blind mice

Row, Row, Row Your Boat

This means 2 strums or beats per measure

Row, Row, Row your boat gent - ly down the stream. Mer - ri - ly, Mer - ri - ly, Mer - ri - ly, Mer - ri - ly life is but a dream.

11

A New Chord

G7

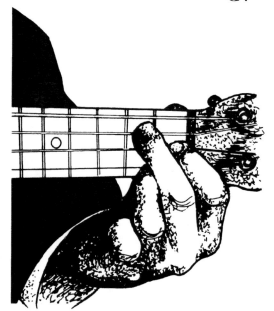

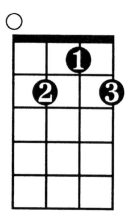

Starting pitch

Skip To My Lou

C
Choose your part - ner skip to my Lou,

G7
Choose your part - ner skip to my Lou,

C
Choose your part - ner skip to my Lou,

G7
Skip to my Lou my dar - ling!

C
Left and Right, Oh skip to my Lou

G7
Left and Right, Oh skip to my Lou

C
Left and Right, Oh skip to my Lou

G7   C
Skip to my Lou my darling.

Rock-A-My Soul

Starting pitch

C

Spiritual

Rock - a - my soul____ in the bo - som of A - bra-ham;

G7

Rock a - my-soul__ in the bo-som of A - bra-ham; Rock-a - my soul in the

bo - som of A - bra - ham; Oh, Rock-a - my soul._____

Polly Wolly Doodle

Starting pitch

Oh I went down South for to see my Sal, sing-ing pol-ly wol- ly doo-dle all the

day, My Sal she is a pret - ty gal, sing-ing

pol - ly wol-ly doo-dle all the day. Fare thee well,__ fare thee well, fare thee

well my fair - y fey, For I'm goin'-to Lou - si - an - a for to

see my Su - si - an - na, Sing-ing pol - ly wol - ly doo - dle all the day.

13

Oh, My Darling Clementine

Three Fishermen

Starting pitch

1. Once there were three fish er - men.
Once there were three fish - er - men. Fish-er, Fish-er, men, men, men.
Fish - er, Fish-er men, men, men. Once there were three Fish - er - men.

vs. 2. First one's name was Abraham
(Repeat)
Abra, Abra, ham, ham, ham
(Repeat)
First one's name was Abraham

vs. 3. Second's name was Isaac.
Isy, Isy, ac, ac, ac.

vs. 5. Wish they'd gone to Amsterdam.
Amster, Amster, dam, dam, dam.

vs. 4. Third one's name was Jacob
Jakey, Jakey, cub, cub, cub.

Pay Me Money Down

Starting pitch

West Indian Folk Song

Chorus Pay me,_ oh, pay me,_ Pay me my mon-ey down,_
Pay me or go to jail,_ Pay me my mon-ey down._

2. I thought I heard the captain say,
Pay me my money down.
Tomorrow is our sailing day,
Pay me my money down.
Chorus

15

Oh Where Has My Little Dog Gone?

Down-Up Strum

/ = Down Strum

V = Up Strum

Down Strum /

Up Strum V

Buffalo Gals

He's Got The Whole World

Starting pitch

2. He's got the little bitsy baby.... 3. He's got you and me brother.....

Hey Lolly

Starting pitch

C
1. Wake up in the mornin', sunny **and** bright
     G7
Hey lolly, lolly lo.
Looked in the mirror, got a terrible fright!
     C
Hey lolly, lolly lo.
C
2. I have a girl she's ten feet tall,
      G7
Hey lolly, lolly lo.
Sleeps on the floor with her feet in the hall,
      C
Hey lolly, lolly lo.

[make up your own verses]

18

The F Chord

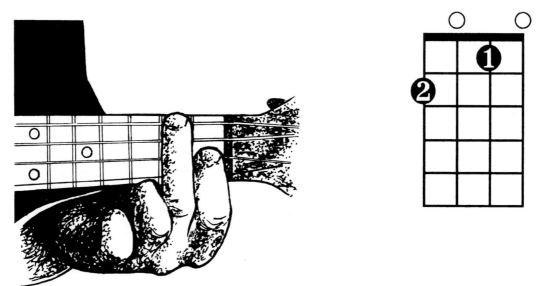

Master the following chord study:

Repeat until no time is lost in changing.

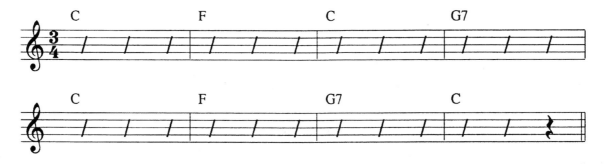

The C, F, and G7 chords are the principal chords in the key of C.

Santa Lucia

Yellow Rose Of Texas

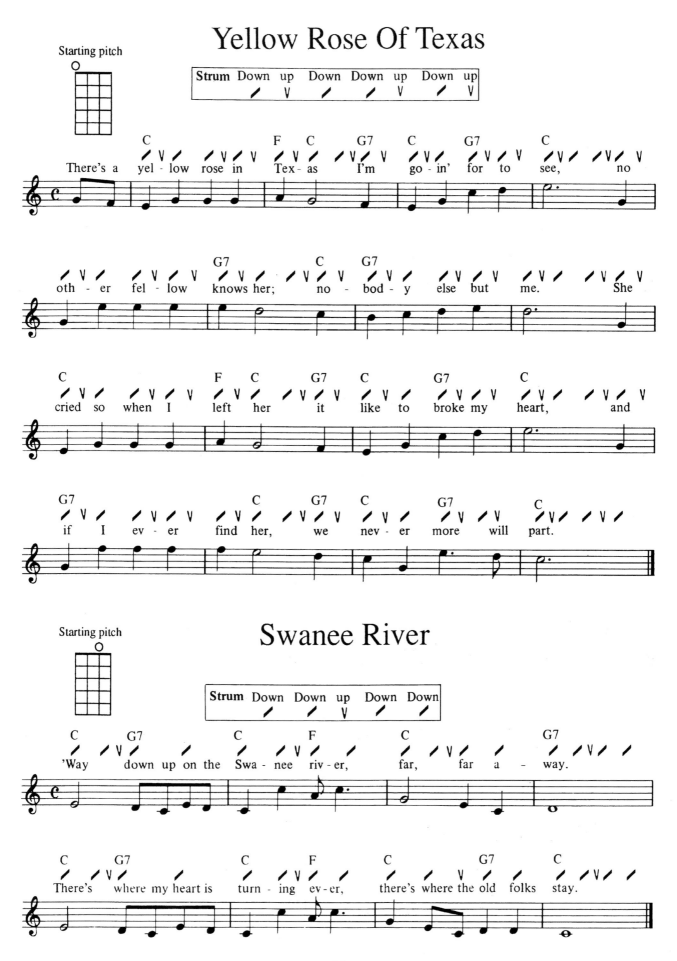

Starting pitch

Strum Down up Down Down up Down up

C · F C G7 C G7 C
There's a yel-low rose in Tex-as I'm go-in' for to see, no

G7 C G7
oth-er fel-low knows her; no-bod-y else but me. She

C F C G7 C G7 C
cried so when I left her it like to broke my heart, and

G7 C G7 C G7 C
if I ev-er find her, we nev-er more will part.

Swanee River

Starting pitch

Strum Down Down up Down Down

C G7 C F C G7
'Way down up on the Swa-nee riv-er, far, far a-way.

C G7 C F C G7 C
There's where my heart is turn-ing ev-er, there's where the old folks stay.

21

Wildwood Flower

Our Boys Will Shine Tonight

The Marine's Hymn

Camptown Races

Railroad Bill

Every Time I Feel The Spirit

Standing In The Need Of Prayer

Two New Chords

The D7 Chord

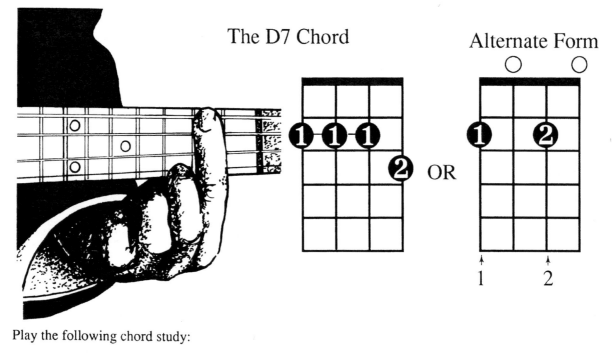

Alternate Form

OR

1   2

Play the following chord study:

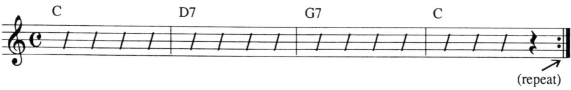

C   D7   G7   C

(repeat)

The G Chord

The chords in the key of G are: G, C, and D7.

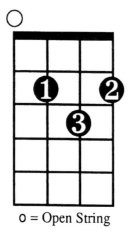

o = Open String

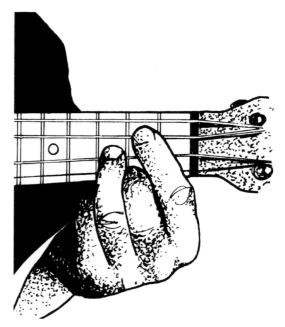

Play the following chord study:

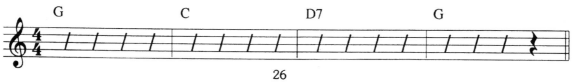

G   C   D7   G

Aloha Oe
(Farewell To Thee)

Moonlight Bay

Go Tell It On The Mountain

Battle Hymn Of The Republic

2. I have seen Him in the watch fires of a hundred circling camps.
They have builded Him an altar in the evening dews and damps.
I have read His righteous sentence by the dim of flaring lamps,
His truth is marching on.

3. In the beauty of the lilies, Christ was born across the sea,
With a glory in His bosom that transfigures you and me;
As He died to make men holy, Let us die to make men free,
While God is marching on.

Away In A Manger

This Little Light Of Mine

Peace Like A River

Starting pitch

Strum	Down	Down	Down	up	Down	up

1. I've got peace like a riv-er, I've got peace like a riv-er, I've got peace like a riv-er in my soul; I've got peace like a riv-er I've got peace like a riv-er, I've got peace like a riv-er in my soul.

2. I've got joy like a fountain

3. I've got love like an ocean.

All Through The Night

Starting pitch

Slowly

Strum	Down	Down	Down	up

Sleep, my child, and peace at-tend thee. All through the night.
Guar-dian an-gels, God will send thee all through the night. *(Repeat)*

Soft and drow-sy hours are creep-ing, hill and vale in slum – ber sleep-ing

I am lov-ing vig-il keep-ing all through the night.

     G   C   D7   C D7   G
2. While the moon her watch is keeping, all through the night.
     G   C   D7   C D7   G
While the weary world is sleeping, all through the night.
     C
O'er thy spirit gently stealing,
        D7
Visions of delight revealing,
     G   C   D7   C D7   G
Breathes a pure and holy feeling, all through the night.

Blow, Ye Winds

The Wabash Cannonball

Down By The Riverside

2. I'm gonna join hands with everyone, etc.
3. I'm gonna put on my long white robe, etc.
4. I'm gonna talk with the **Prince of Peace, etc.**

She'll Be Coming Round The Mountain

The Gospel Train

2. The fare is cheap and all can go,
The rich and poor are there;
No second class aboard this train,
No difference in the fare. Chorus

3. I hear that train a-comin',
She sure is speedin' fast,
So get your tickets ready
And ride to heaven at last. Chorus

35

Chords In The Key Of D

The three primary chords in the key of D are: D, G, and A7.

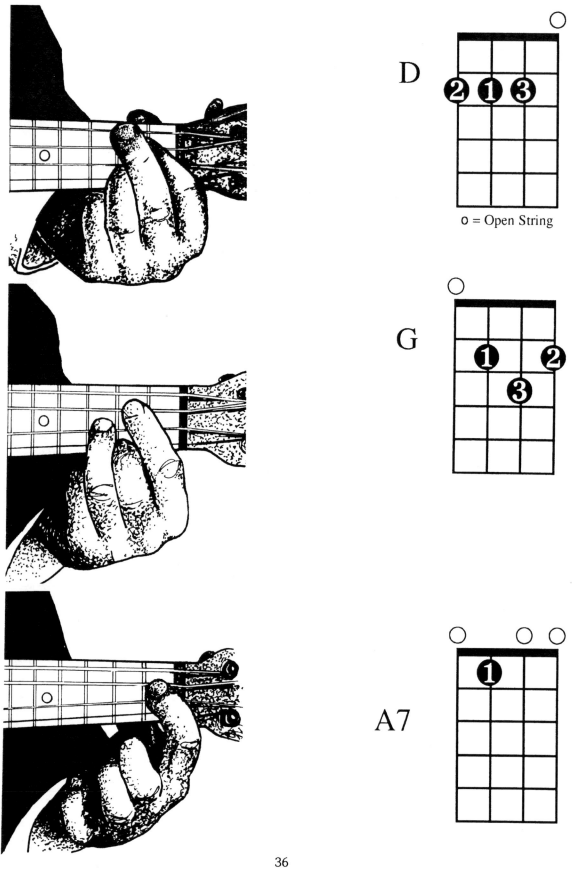

D

o = Open String

G

A7

She Wore A Yellow Ribbon

Starting pitch

Strum	Down	Down	up	Down	Down
	/	/	V	/	/

American
Folk Song

Bright Tempo

D
But, in her heart, she has a secret passion
                              A7
She has it in the springtime, and in the month of May;
D
And if you asked her who is now her passion,
                             A7   **D**
She has it for a college man who's not so far away.
    Chorus

37

When The Saints Go Marchin' In

2. And when they gather 'round the throne.
3. And when they crown him **King** of kings
4. And on that Hallelujah day.

Streets Of Laredo

2. "Go fetch me a cup, a cup of cold water,
To cool my parched lips," the cowboy then said;
Before I returned, the spirit had left him
And gone to its Maker - the cowboy was dead.

3. We beat the drum slowly and played the fife lowly,
And bitterly wept as we bore him along;
For we all loved our comrade, so brave, young, and handsome,
We all loved our comrade although he'd done wrong.

Crawdad Song

39

The Girl I Left Behind Me

Li'l Liza Jane

Oh! Susanna

Come And Go With Me

2. There'll be singin' in that land
3. There'll be dancin' in that land.
4. There is freedom in that land
5. There is love in that land.

Frankie & Johnny

Chords In The Key of F

The three primary chords in the key of F are: F, B♭, and C7.

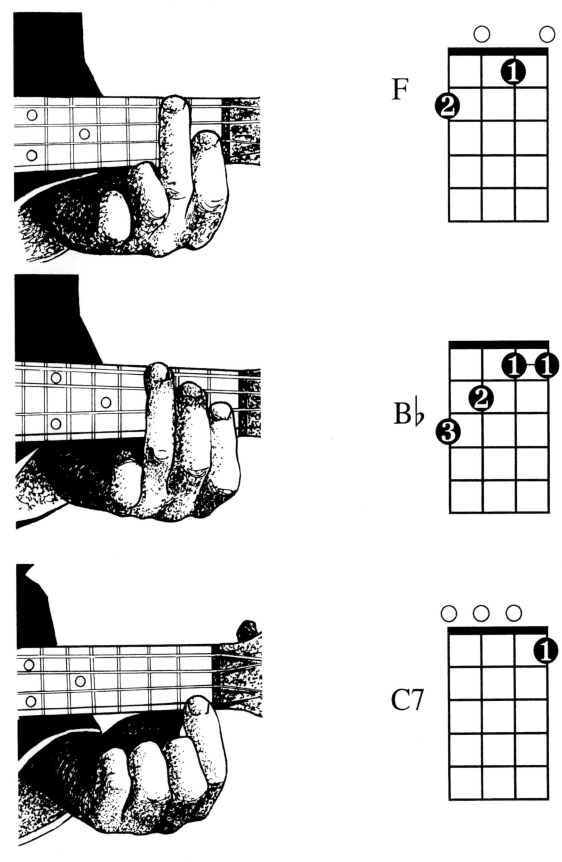

Juanita

2. When in thy dreaming moons like these shall shine again,
   And daylight beaming prove thy dreams are vain,
   Wilt thou not, relenting, for thine absent lover sigh?
   In thy heart consenting to a prayer gone by?
   Nita! Juanita! Let me linger by thy side!
   Nita! Juanita! Be my own fair bride.

44

Swing Low, Sweet Chariot

Starting pitch

2. When I get to glory, my voice I'll raise,
Comin' for to carry me home,
To sing a song of grateful praise,
Comin' for to carry me home.

This Train

47

Beautiful Brown Eyes

Goin' Down The Road Feelin' Bad

48

More Advanced Songs
Key of C

Fascination

CHORDS Needed:

Chinatown, My Chinatown

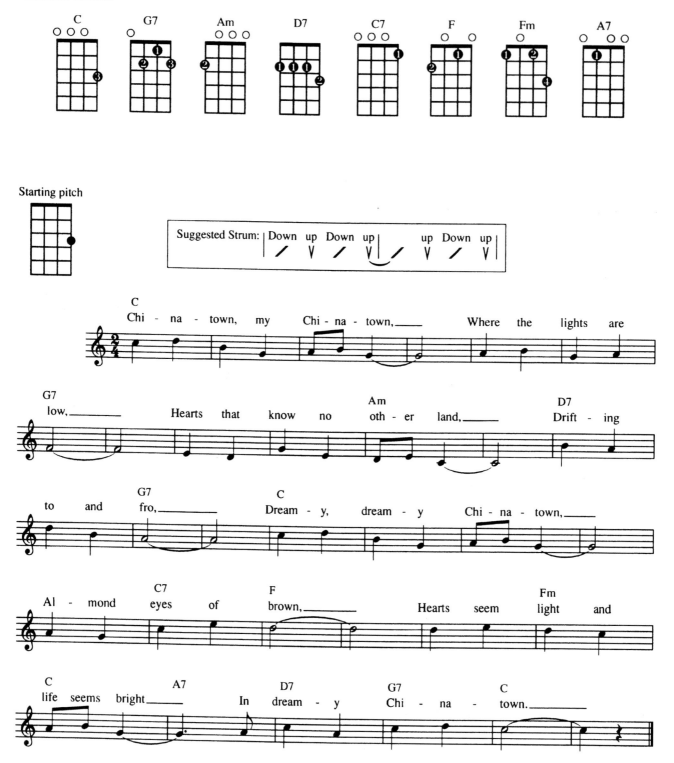

Ida, Sweet As Apple Cider

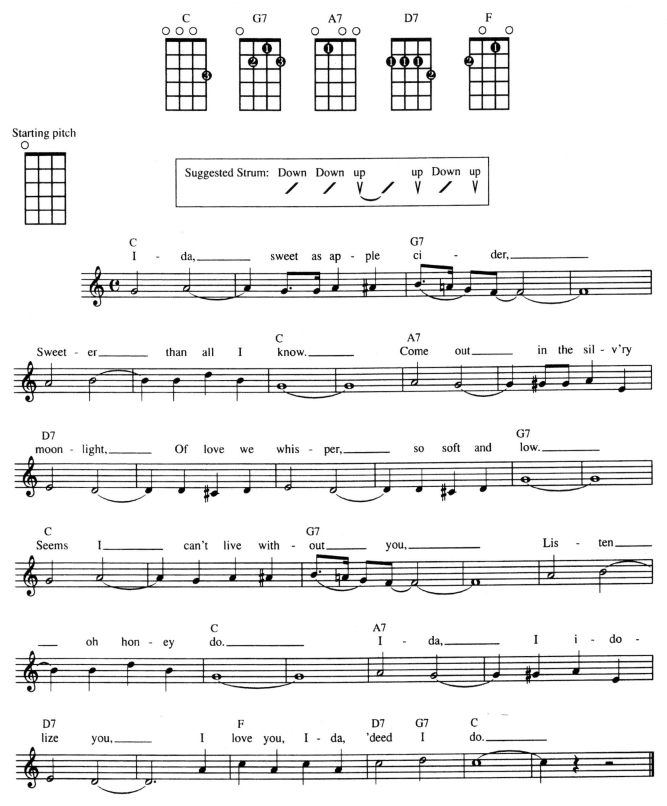

When Irish Eyes Are Smiling

By the Light of the Silvery Moon

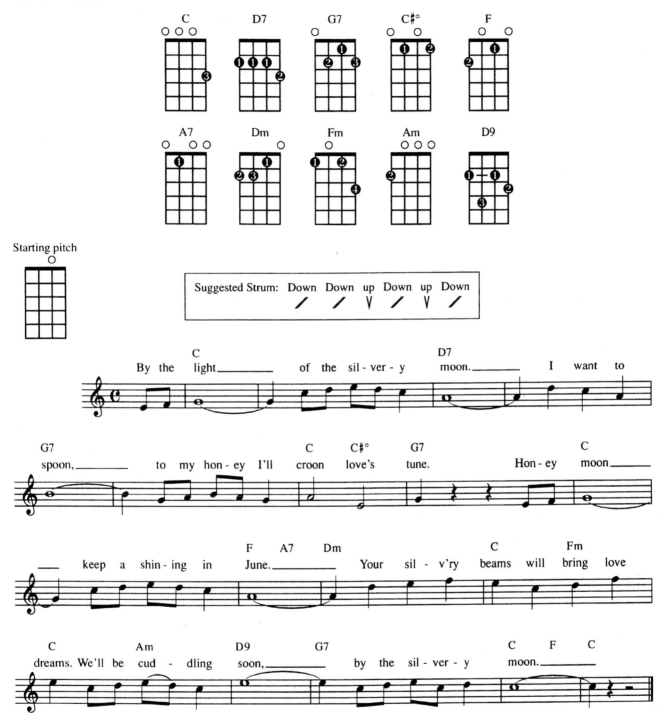

The Darktown Strutters' Ball

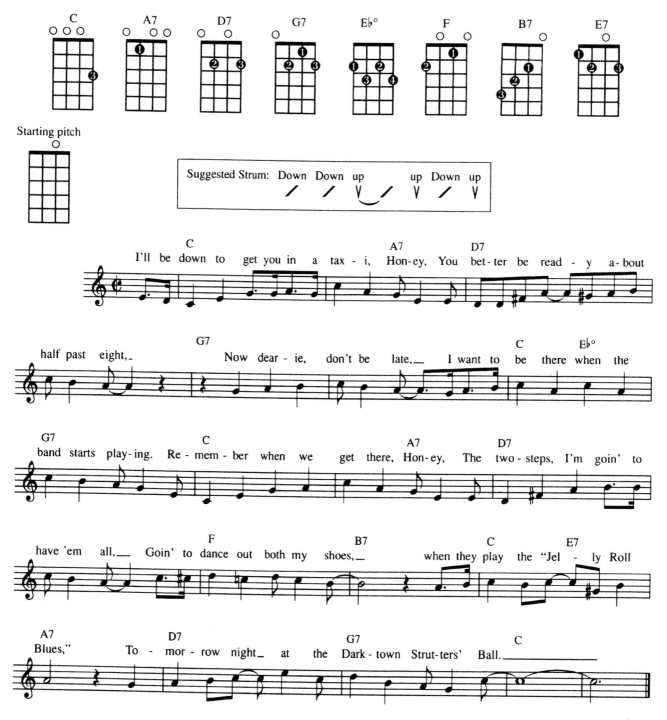

CHORDS Needed:

Starting pitch

Suggested Strum: Down Down up up Down up

C I'll be down to get you in a tax-i, Hon-ey, **A7** You bet-ter be read-y **D7** a-bout

half past eight,__ **G7** Now dear-ie, don't be late,__ I want to be there **C** when the **Eb°**

G7 band starts play-ing. Re-mem-ber when we get there, Hon-ey, **A7** The two-steps, I'm **D7** goin' to

have 'em all,__ **F** Goin' to dance out both my shoes,__ **B7** when they play the **C** "Jel - **E7** ly Roll

A7 Blues," **D7** To - mor - row night__ at the **G7** Dark - town Strut-ters' Ball. **C** _____

That's An Irish Lullaby

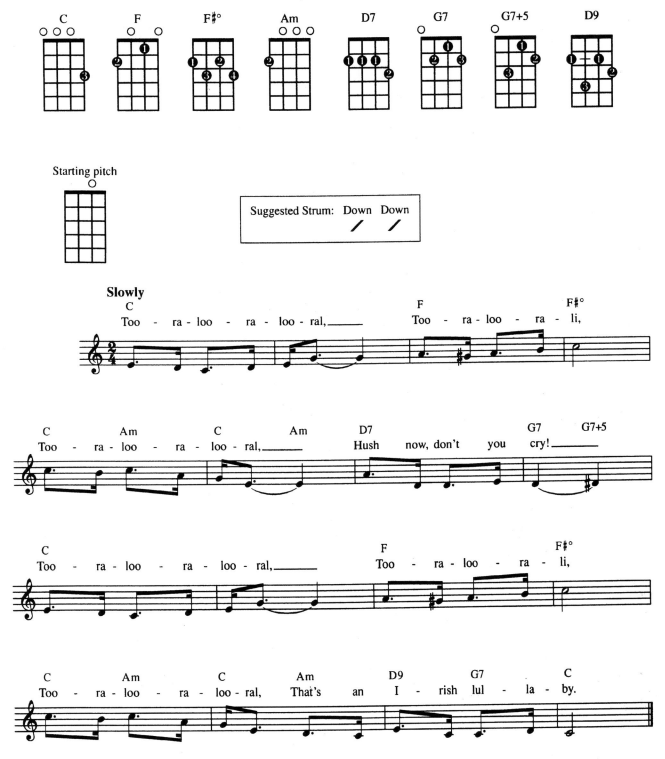

Meet Me In St. Louis, Louis

Dear Old Girl

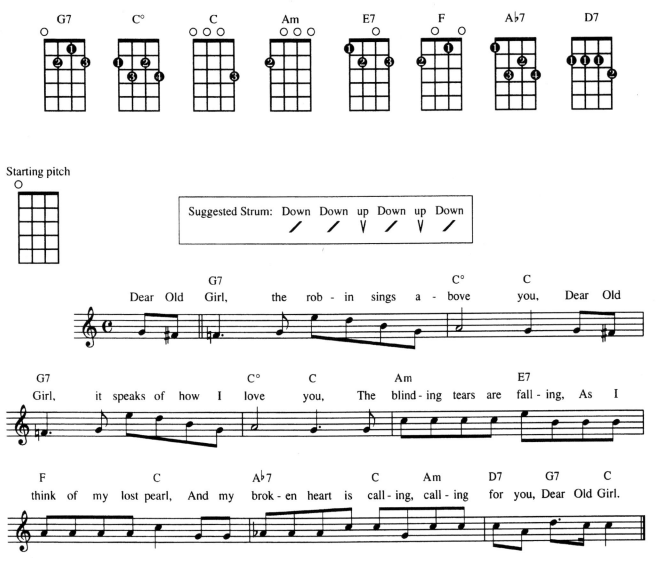

CHORDS Needed:

Starting pitch

Suggested Strum: Down Down up Down up Down

G7   C°   C
Dear Old Girl, the rob - in sings a - bove you, Dear Old

G7   C°   C   Am   E7
Girl, it speaks of how I love you, The blind - ing tears are fall - ing, As I

F   C   A♭7   C   Am   D7   G7   C
think of my lost pearl, And my brok - en heart is call - ing, call - ing for you, Dear Old Girl.

In My Merry Oldsmobile

Shine On Harvest Moon

The Sidewalks of New York
[East Side, West Side]

Wait Till The Sun Shines, Nellie

CHORDS Needed:

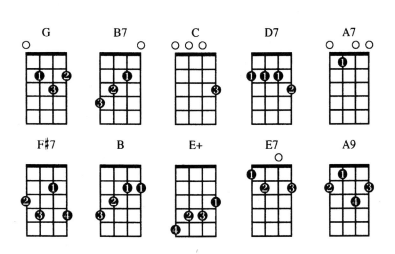

Starting pitch

Suggested Strum: Down Down Down up Down up

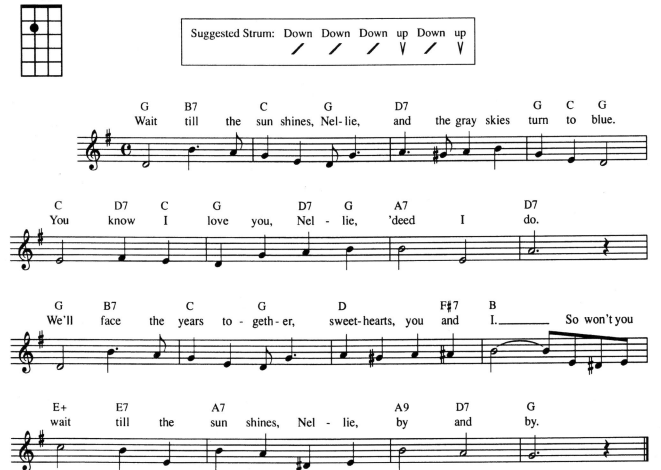

G B7 C G D7 G C G
Wait till the sun shines, Nel-lie, and the gray skies turn to blue.

C D7 C G D7 G A7 D7
You know I love you, Nel-lie, 'deed I do.

G B7 C G D F#7 B
We'll face the years to-geth-er, sweet-hearts, you and I._____ So won't you

E+ E7 A7 A9 D7 G
wait till the sun shines, Nel-lie, by and by.

Down By The Old Mill Stream

While Strolling Through The Park One Day

Bill Bailey, Won't You Please Come Home?

For Me And My Gal

Oh, You Beautiful Doll

CHORDS Needed:

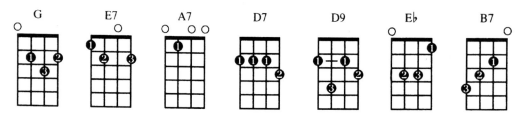

Starting pitch

I Wonder Who's Kissing Her Now

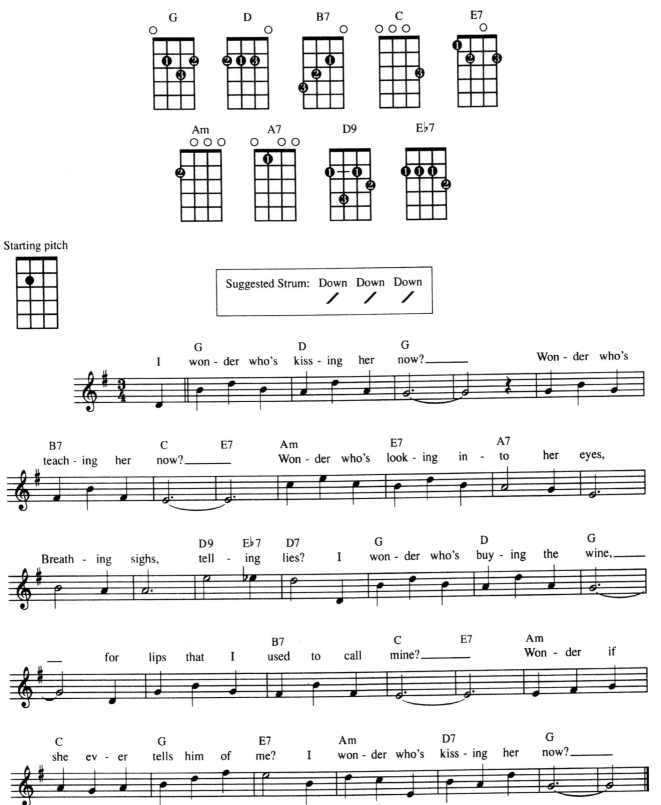

I Want A Girl

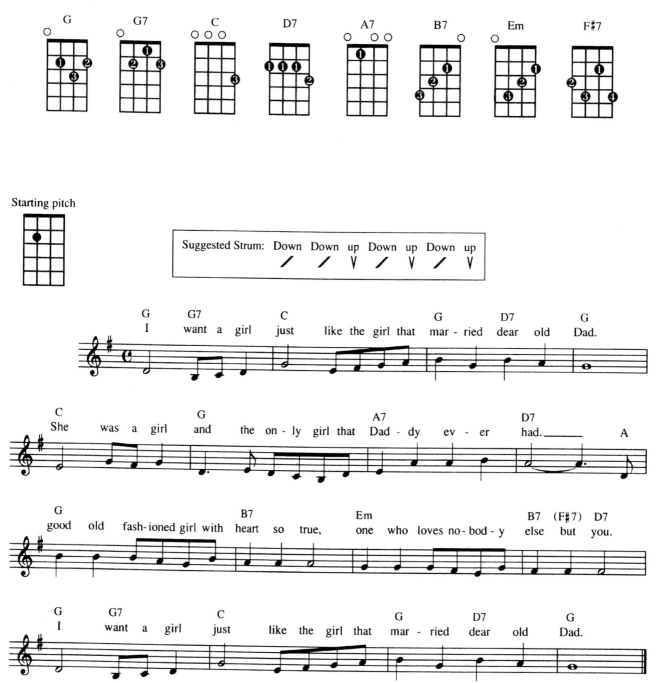

Poor Butterfly

Key of F

When You And I Were Young, Maggie

CHORDS Needed:

Starting pitch

Suggested Strum: Down Down up Down Down up

F / Bb / F
I___ wan-dered to-day to the hill, Maggie, To watch the___ scene be -

C7 / F / Bb / F / C7
low, The___ creek and the old rust-y mill, Mag-gie, where we sat in the long,___ long a -

F / Bb / Gm7 / F / C / G7
go. The green grove is gone from the hill, Mag-gie, Where first the dai - sies___

C / C7 / F / Bb / F / C7 / F
sprung; The old rust-y mill is___ still Maggie, since you and___ I were___ young.

Hello! Ma Baby

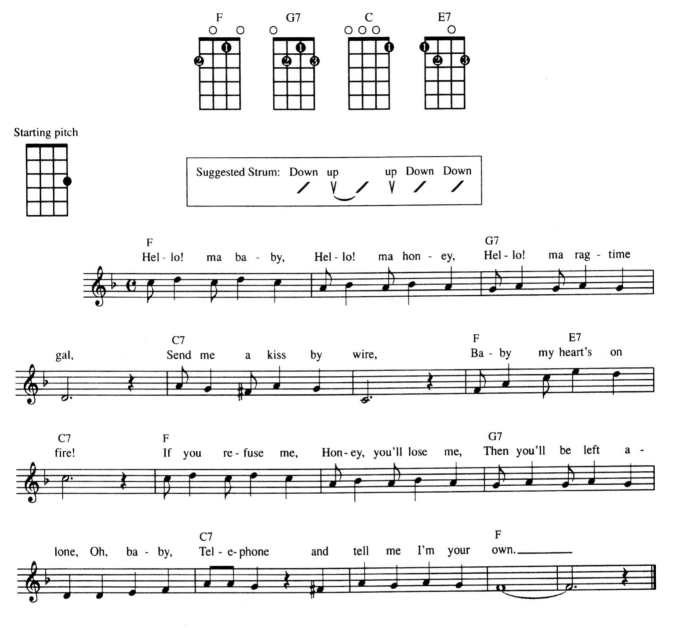

Melody of Love

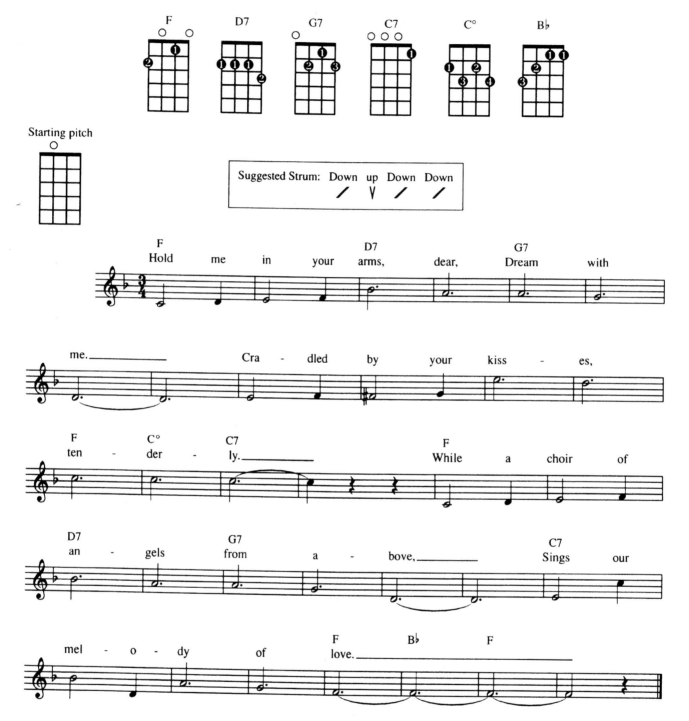

Alexander's Ragtime Band

CHORDS Needed:

Starting pitch

Suggested Strum: Down up Down up Down up Down up

F   D   C7

Come on and hear,____ come on and hear Al - ex - an - der's rag - time

F   F+   Bb

band.____ Come on and hear,____ come on and hear. It's the best band in the land. They can

F

play a bu - gle call like you nev - er heard be - fore, So nat - ur - al that you want to go to war.

C   G7   C7   F

That's just the best - est band what am, hon - ey lamb. Come on a - long,____ come on a -

D   C7   F   F+   Bb

long. Let me take you by the hand,____ up to the man,____ up to the man who's the

F   F7   Bb

lead - er of the band.____ And if you care to hear the Swa - nee Riv - er played in

G#°   F   C7   F

rag - time,__ come on and hear,____ come on and hear____ Al - ex - an - der's rag - time band.

After the Ball

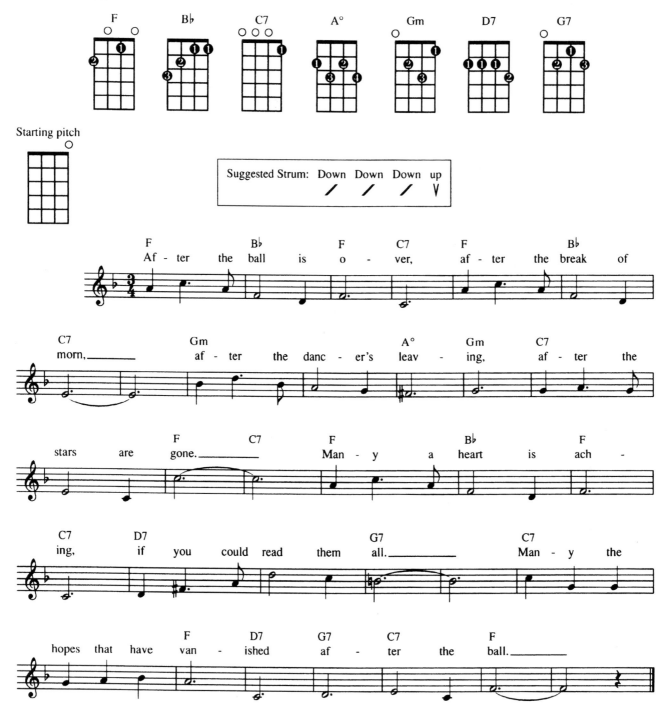

I Love You Truly

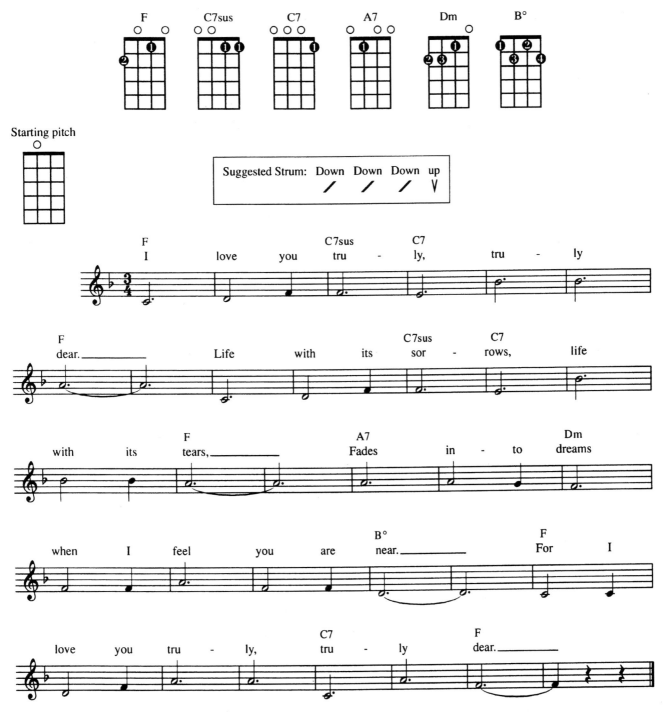

You're A Grand Old Flag

CHORDS Needed:

F   Bb   C7   A7   Dm   G7   D7   Gm

Starting pitch

Suggested Strum: | Down Down | Down Down up |

You're a grand old flag, you're a high fly-ing flag and for-ev-er in peace may you wave._____ You're the em-blem of the land I love, the home of the free and the brave._____ Ev-'ry heart beats true 'neath the red, white and blue, where there's nev-er a boast or brag._____ But should auld ac-quaint-ance be for-got, keep your eye on the grand old flag._____

Bicycle Built For Two

CHORDS Needed:

Starting pitch

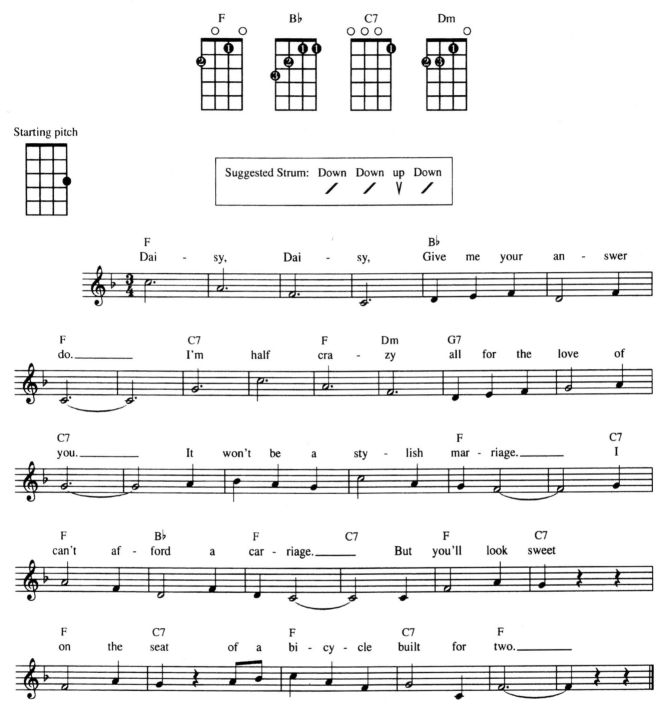

Alabama Jubilee

Sweet Rosie O'Grady

Peg O' My Heart

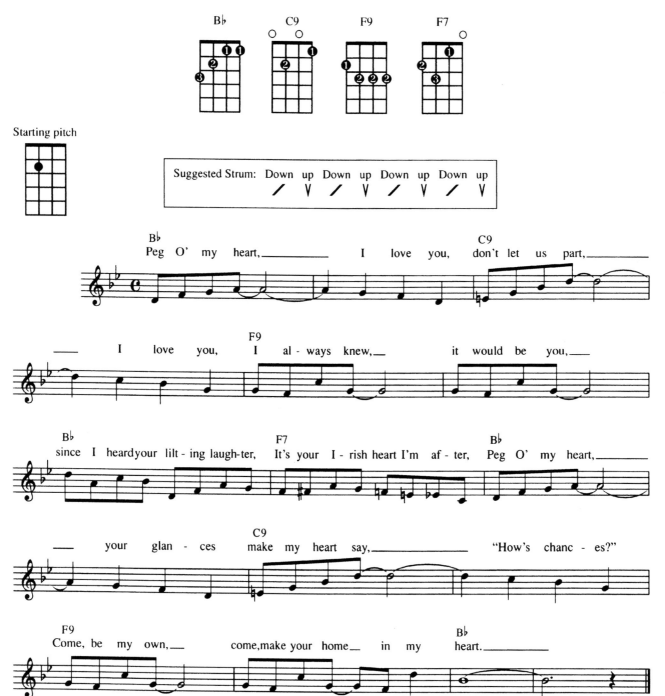

Ballin' The Jack

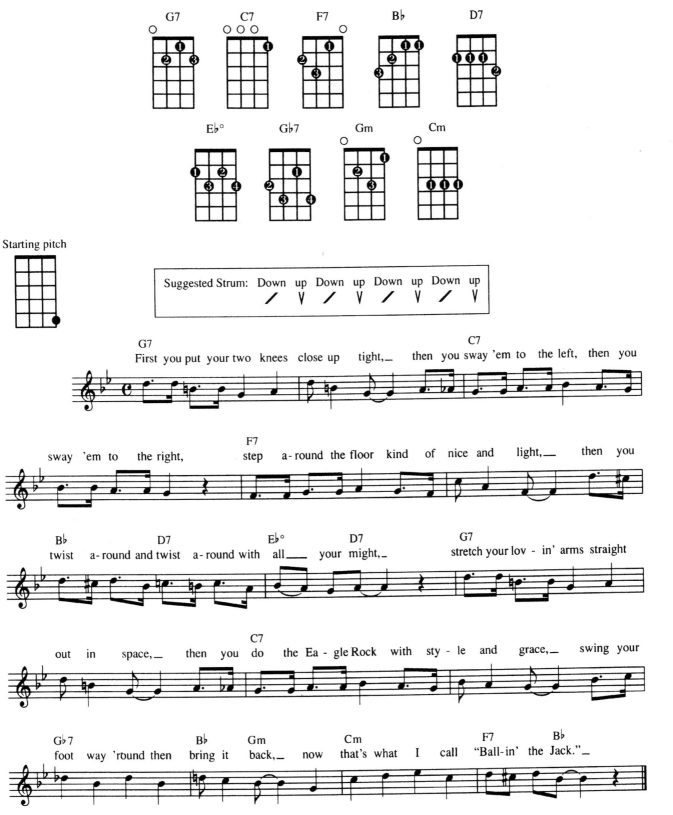

In The Good Old Summertime

CHORDS Needed:

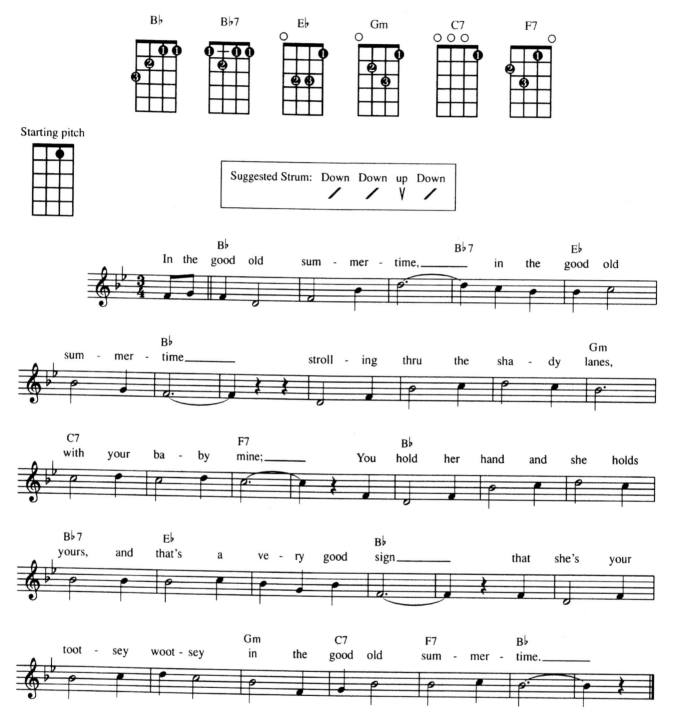

Starting pitch

Suggested Strum: Down Down up Down

In the good old sum - mer - time,_____ in the good old

sum - mer - time_____ stroll - ing thru the sha - dy lanes,

with your ba - by mine;_____ You hold her hand and she holds

yours, and that's a ve - ry good sign_____ that she's your

toot - sey woot - sey in the good old sum - mer - time._____

The Yankee Doodle Boy

CHORDS Needed:

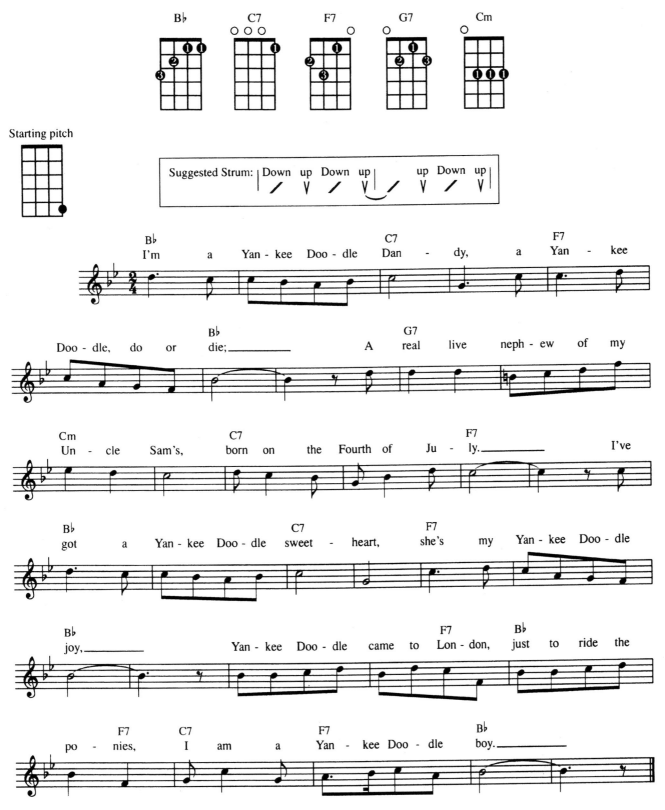

My Gal Sal

My Wild Irish Rose

CHORDS Needed:

Starting pitch

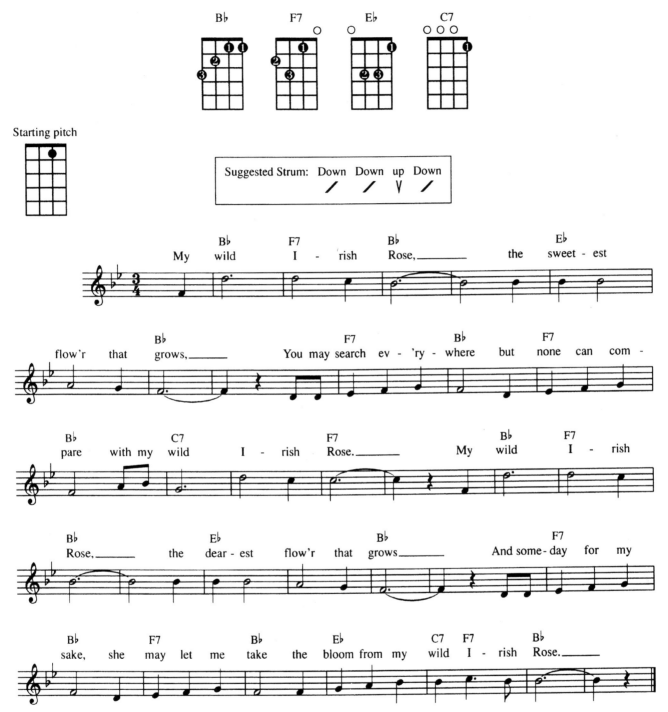

Give My Regards To Broadway

CHORDS Needed:

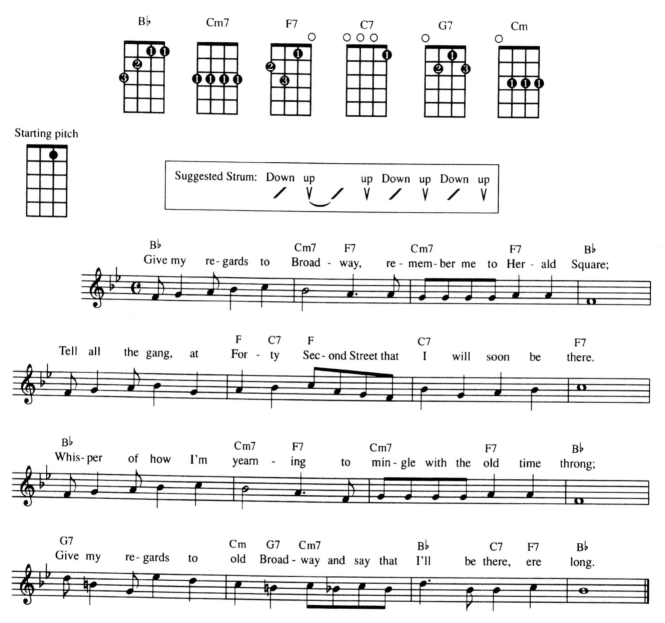

Starting pitch

Suggested Strum: Down up   up Down up Down up

Bb   Cm7   F7   Cm7   F7   Bb
Give my re-gards to Broad - way, re - mem-ber me to Her - ald Square;

F   C7   F   C7   F7
Tell all the gang, at For - ty Sec - ond Street that I will soon be there.

Bb   Cm7   F7   Cm7   F7   Bb
Whis- per of how I'm yearn - ing to min - gle with the old time throng;

G7   Cm G7 Cm7   Bb   C7 F7   Bb
Give my re- gards to old Broad - way and say that I'll be there, ere long.

Take Me Out To The Ballgame

Let Me Call You Sweetheart

Key of D

The Blue Bells of Scotland

CHORDS Needed:

Starting pitch

Suggested Strum: Down Down up Down Down

Oh where, and oh where is your___ High - land lad - die gone?

Oh where, and oh where is your___ High - land lad - die gone?

He's gone to fight the foe for King___ George up - on the throne.

And it's oh! In my heart, how I___ wish him safe at home!

Over the River and Through the Woods

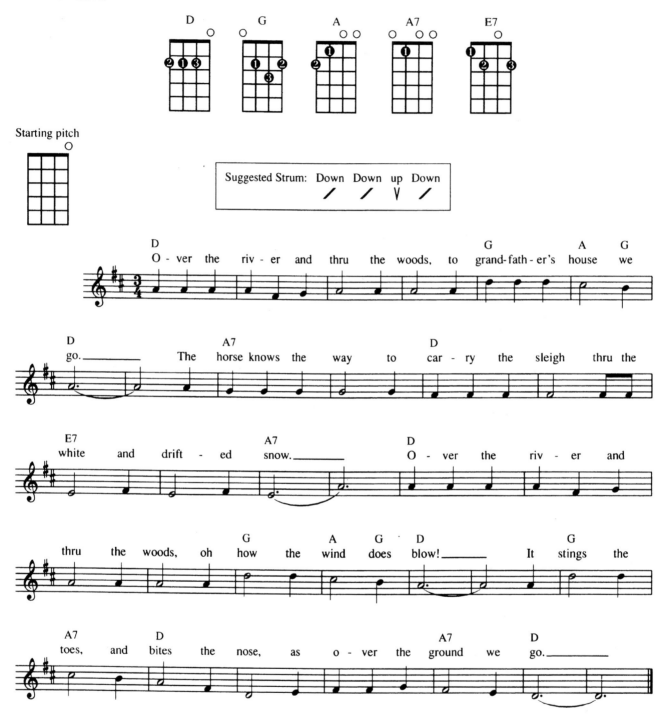

Beautiful Dreamer

Pretty Baby

My Melancholy Baby

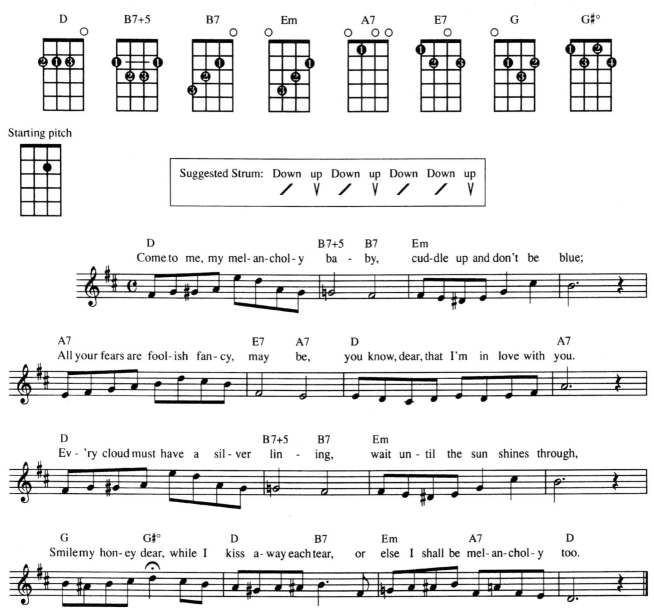

Basic Uke Chord Chart

MAJOR Chords

C   F   G   D   A   E

Bb   Eb   Ab   Db   Gb/F#   B

MINOR Chords

Cm   Fm   Gm   Dm   Am   Em

Bbm   Ebm   Abm   Dbm   Gbm/F#m   Bm

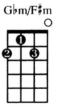

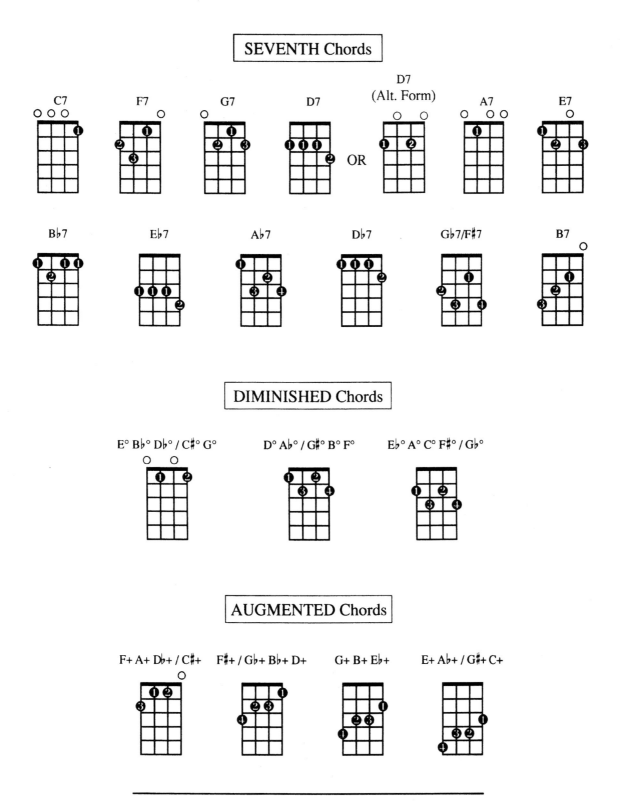

SEVENTH Chords

DIMINISHED Chords

AUGMENTED Chords

For complete Photo/Diagram Chord Listing see

Mel Bay's Ukulele Chord Book (MB 93269)

Index Of Songs